ISBN 978-0-483-01547-0
PIBN 10053325

This book is a reproduction of an important historical work. Forgotten Books uses
state-of-the-art technology to digitally reconstruct the work, preserving the original format
whilst repairing imperfections present in the aged copy. In rare cases, an imperfection in
the original, such as a blemish or missing page, may be replicated in our edition. We do,
however, repair the vast majority of imperfections successfully; any imperfections that
remain are intentionally left to preserve the state of such historical works.

THE POLITICAL SITUATION

SITUATION

BY

OLIVE SCHREINER

AND

C. S. CRONWRIGHT-SCHREINER

London

T. FISHER UNWIN

1896

*A Paper read by S. C. Cronwright-Schrei
in the Town Hall, Kimberley,
August 20, 1895.*

Two questions force themselves upon us when looking at our political situation in the Cape Colony to-day.

Firstly: What is the cause of that steady and persistent Retrogressive Movement which has marked our political existence during the last years?

Secondly: How is that Retrogressive Movement to be stayed?

PART I.

PART I.

LET us glance first at the conditions of this Retrogressive Movement, and see if its cause be discoverable.

That such a movement has taken place admits of no doubt.

Many of the measures passed have not only shown no tendency to accord with the movement known as Liberal or Progressive in all countries inhabited by Europeans; but they have shown a persistent tendency to move in a contrary direction, and even to undo the more advanced and progressive legislative enactments of the past.

RETROGRESSIVE LEGISLATION.

While in all civilised countries where representative institutions prevail the tendency is to move without intermission in the direction of a broadened electoral basis, so that in several of the English colonies to-day we find manhood suffrage, or one man one vote, or adult suffrage ; and while even the most backward of European countries are rapidly tending year by year towards these conditions—we, I believe, alone among civilised people have deliberately, during the last few years, narrowed our basis,[1] and undone the progressive work of the last generation.

So also while in all enlightened countries during the past sixty years public opinion has been steadily advancing in the direction of doing away with the lash as a punishment for minor offences, we in this country have not only, during the last years, possessed certain individuals in our Legislative

[1] The Franchise Act, introduced and voted for unanimously by the last Ministry, Mr. Rhodes being Premier, raised the monetary qualification from £25 to £75 per annum.

Councils who have striven to introduce an Act making legal the infliction of corporal punishment for the smallest offences towards master or mistress on the part of household or other servants, and which, if passed would be merely a recurrence to slavery under a new name—but this Act was voted for by three members in the last Ministry, two of them being Englishmen, and one the Premier, Mr. Cecil Rhodes.

Again, while in all civilised countries the tendency, as each country advances, is to consider more and more the welfare of its labouring classes ; to remove oppressive restrictions ; to endeavour by every lawful means to increase their wages ; and to regard the labourer, not merely as a means for increasing the wealth of other sections of the community, but to legislate for *his* welfare, and to regard *his* happiness as one of the pressing considerations of the State—we in this country have, under the Glen Grey Act of last year, brought in and supported by Mr. Cecil Rhodes and his following, an enactment which compels even the self-supporting and industrious native to work for the white man for a certain time every year, whether he will or no ; laying himself open to imprisonment or fine if he refuse, even though his going out to labour for the white man should entail the neglect of his own cultivated lands.

So again, with regard to land tenure ; while in all progressive countries there is a tendency to obtain and retain as large a part as possible of lands, mines, and great public works as the property of, and to be worked for the benefit of, the nation as a whole—we, in this country, are for ever and completely alienating our public lands, our minerals, our precious stones, and even our public works.

And further, not only are we alienating them within our own

boundaries, and allowing almost without a struggle a small band of Monopolists to gain possession and control of that wealth which should be ours and our children's to employ for the benefit of the nation that shall be, but we are enabling them to grasp adjacent territories still uninhabited by the white man, so that when the mass of civilised men shall enter into occupation there, they will find nothing of value left for themselves in that state which, by their labour, they will have to build up ; the alien will already have set his grasp upon all that is fair or rich. For not as in other countries has the Monopolist risen up among us, a growth of our own ; he comes from a foreign clime, and sweeps bare the virgin land before him like the locust ; and, like the locust, leaves nothing for his successors but the barren earth.

While in New Zealand and other advanced colonies every legislative effort is being made to retain the land for the people, we are quietly allowing ourselves to be stripped bare session after session, and are confiding our possession into the hands of the Speculator and Monopolist.

Lastly, while in enlightened countries there is a continually increasing tendency to raise the revenue, not by taxing the primary necessaries of life, upon which almost the whole income of the labouring classes is necessarily expended, but to raise it through the taxation of luxuries, whether by means of Excise or Import dues, we in this country find that not only are our necessaries of life already taxed to an appalling extent,[1] but a heavy additional tax on wheat and flour, and an almost prohibitive tax on imported meat,[2] is being levied upon

[1] For instance, wheat 38 per cent., flour 59 per cent., unrefined sugar 107 per cent., butter 20 per cent., cheese 43 per cent., candles 59 per cent., paraffin 202 per cent.

[2] Frozen meat 2d. per lb., wheat an additional 38 per cent.

us ; while diamonds (forming a monopoly of which the Prime Minister is the head) and the intoxicating liquors, inferior in quality, so largely produced in this country, are allowed to go untaxed.

So also in small matters.

In Australia, where the material welfare of the country largely depends on its wool, it has been clearly seen that to allow the land to be partially ruined by the existence of an easily eradicated disease in the stock was scandalous and immoral ; and they have legislated so successfully that in certain Australian colonies the insect which causes the disease has been exterminated. It has been felt in those countries that the man who refuses to exterminate scab in his flocks inflicts a merciless wrong and injustice upon his fellows whose flocks his own infect ; and the Australians have, by stringent legislation, made such conduct impossible.

It is not necessary to say that in this country all attempts to legislate in defence of the man who endeavours to keep his flocks healthy have been crushed or emasculated.

Many other matters will suggest themselves to every one in which our legislation has shown this retrograde tendency. We have no time now to enter into details with regard to such measures as Haarhoff's Bill, which, as introduced, was intended to make it culpable for any aboriginal native, whether a domestic servant, householder, newspaper editor, or clergyman, to be found walking on pavements in our towns ; and also to make it punishable for any aboriginal native to be found out of doors within a township after nine o'clock at night unless he or she had been given a pass by the Magistrate or other authorised person—a Bill which also received the support of the existing Government.

On the whole, it is evident that no impartial mind can

look at the course of our legislation during recent years without realising the fact that while the wheels of legislation in other civilised and Anglo-Saxon communities are tending to propel the car of state forwards, ours are slowly but surely running us backwards.

RETROGRESSIVE FACTORS : I. THE BOND.

Now, when we turn to inquire of ourselves what the reason of this Retrogressive Movement may be, I think the superficial reply, given when we glance merely at the surface of our public life, would be this : that the Retrogressive

Movement of late years has been entirely the work of that organisation known throughout South Africa as the Afrikander Bond ; and which has in recent years attained to such influence that it apparently coerces Ministry after Ministry, bending them to its will. But a deeper examination will, I think, show us that the Bond alone would not have been able to produce this movement. Another influence, working into the hands of the Bond, has given it for a moment the power of forcing this retrogression upon the country.

But before we turn to consider this secondary influence,

let us glance at the Bond itself.

The Afrikander Bond was in its origin one of the most beneficent and desirable institutions that have appeared in South Africa. It banded together, and aroused to healthy interest in the affairs of the State, a large body of men who, hitherto unorganised and isolated, had not taken that share in the government of the State which their numbers would have justified, and who were therefore unduly disregarded and possibly even unjustly dealt with.

Started originally (as was inevitable under the circumstances) as a more or less racial organisation, and opposing Boer as Boer to Englishman as Englishman, this tone, nevertheless, as time passed, quickly modified itself. To-day the organisation is merely an organisation which draws together and unites for common purposes a number of the early colonists and others holding certain views on social and political matters, and in no way is it a merely racial organisation. To this extent it forms a healthy and desirable element in our public life. Left to itself, and having no adventitious power given it by an extraneous intervention, I believe that, so far from being an evil, the existence of the

Bond would awaken and maintain that healthy friction and interaction of opposing views which is necessary to keep pure and healthy the stream of political life.

But what has this extraneous influence been which has acted upon the Bond, removing it from its healthy position, and enabled it to obtain for the moment an undue power of enforcing its retrogressive views and methods upon the whole Cape Colony?

To explain this influence it will be necessary to examine carefully the nature and power of that small band of Monopolists to whom we before referred.

Africa Before the Monopolists.

South Africa is a country of vast resources. In spite of the dryness of much of our climate, the rocky nature of certain tracts of our soil, taking the whole of South Africa together from east to west, I do not hesitate to assert that not many countries equally desirable and suitable for human habitation will be found. More than a compensation for the dryness of our climate is the absence of the numbing cold of extreme northern and southern lands, which for months in the year renders outdoor labour difficult;

yet more important is the absence of that moist heat which in tropical countries renders exertion almost impossible to the white man, and exhaustive to the dark. A country with temperate, stimulating climate, which favours the health and energy of Europeans, physically and mentally ; which is favourable to the constitution of every species of domestic animal, and is adapted to the cultivation of almost every plant of the temperate and tropical zones ; which, above all, is one of the richest, if not the richest, country in the world in precious stones and minerals of all kinds, and which was originally peopled only by barbarians—this country has always been attractive to Europeans. For 200 years, Boer and Englishman, we have been populating and steadily taking possession of the land, moving steadily northwards. Our progress has not been made by a series of world-striking *coups d'état*, it has been slow, but it has been the more healthy, the more sure, the more deeply rooted, because of its gradual and natural development.

Those superb pioneers of South Africa, its Boers, have continued to move, as they have always moved, northward : our English colonists have been steadily building up their villages, founding their educational institutions, and establishing a liberal and progressive Government. We have not exhausted or even yet opened up many of the mineral resources of our country ; they are still here for the use of our own and future generations ; but so far as the colonists, Dutch and English, have populated the land, our progress, though slow, has been wholesome ; and the land as a whole has been kept free from many of those crushing evils which afflict the older civilisations of Europe, and even affect some of the younger dependencies.

There is a sense in which we

have been a poor people. We have had no mass of surplus wealth wrung from the labour of a working class, but we have been a very rich people, perhaps one of the richest on the earth, in the fact that grinding poverty, and the enormous and superfluous wealth of individuals, were equally unknown among us. Our people as a whole led a simple but comfortable life ; our labouring classes were engaged in no unhealthy occupation ; starvation and want were unknown among us ; we were progressing steadily, if slowly, and keeping our national wealth for the people as a whole, and for all who should labour among us.

But a new element has burst into South African life.

RETROGRESSIVE FACTORS:
II. THE MONOPOLIST.

When diamonds were first discovered here, in the true old South African manner, the find was considered as one for the people at large. For years there flocked to the Diamond-fields colonists from every part of the country, and the wealth discovered went back to the homes of the people. That wealth rebuilt many a Colonial homestead; it educated many a Colonial child; it enabled landowners to carry out improvements otherwise impos-

sible ; it saved from insolvency
many a Colonial firm which
had sent members to dig ; it
spread throughout the country
a glow of well-being, owing to
the general diffusion in small
sums of the wealth made by
South Africa from the diamonds.
Something analogous took place
in the early days at the Transvaal gold-fields ; and gold-dig-
ging has never yet become quite
so complete a monopoly in the
hands of a few as the diamond
industry.

Time forbids that I should
enter into a detailed account
of the way in which these industries passed from their early
and healthy condition ; the

facts are well known to you all. There were in South Africa certain men from Europe, of great shrewdness, and with large abilities for speculation, who saw at once the possibilities our natural industries opened out before them. The many small original possessors of the wealth of South Africa were not men of vast means, and were rather hard workers than sharp financial speculators ; and the keen-sighted strangers quickly discerned that, could they buy out the small interests one by one and then amalgamate among themselves, slowly but surely the wealth of the country would pass into their hands.

It needed no vast capital to buy out the original possessors.

To-day a small, resolute, and keen body of men, amalgamated into Rings and Trusts, are quickly and surely setting their hands round the mineral wealth of South Africa. Our diamonds are already a complete monopoly in their hands ; our gold, our coal, the richest portions of our soil, and even our public works, are tending to fall into the grasp of our great amalgamators. Not only are these men not South Africans by birth, which would in itself matter nothing, but in the majority of cases they are men who regard South Africa merely as a field for the making of wealth and the furthering of their own designs. When they have attained their end they do not feel themselves bound to the spot which has enriched them, but in most cases retire to Europe to expend the wealth of South Africa in the purchase of social distinction and in the luxuries of old-world life, or in further increasing their command over South African resources.

And South Africa grows poorer !

Yet, were this all, we should be inclined to say, What ground have we for complaint ? These men are but taking advantage of that competitive system which we to-day still uphold. If the men of South Africa are not skilled enough in the methods of gathering together the wealth of a people; and if they have not that fellow-feeling to be able to defeat them, which would enable them to combine, and so retain the land for the people at large; can we blame the men who take advantage of our ignorance and disunion? They are but carrying out their operations on the most approved financial principles! In truth, were this all, we should merely be suffering in a most exaggerated degree from a disease common to many other countries.

THE UNION OF THE TWO FACTORS.

But our evil has not stopped here. Owing to the mental capacity of some of these speculators, and to certain conditions in South African public life, the conception suggested itself to them : that were it possible to obtain complete control of the political machinery in any African State (notably of the Cape Colony), and could they hold the reins of Government in their own hands, their power for increasing their wealth, for resisting taxation upon those industries of which they possessed monopolies, and for extending their commercial exploitations into adjoining territories, would be immeasurably increased.

This conception has been seized and carried out.

The means of its accomplishment in the Cape Colony has been through the complete control gained by the Monopolists over the only group in South Africa whom they could hope to guide, and whom, in view of their extra-colonial plans, it was necessary to keep pacified and well in hand.

It is this command of the political machinery of the country by the Monopolist, owing to his union with one section, which constitutes the real disease from which the Cape Colony is suffering. It is this which lies at the back of our Retrogressive Movement.

For the Monopolist Party, determined to obtain control of the political machinery, could only do so by purchasing the co-operation of some truly South African body. The more shrewd and modern sec-tion of South Africans—pro-fessional men, merchants, go-ahead newspaper-reading far-mers—are, very many of them, unpurchasable ; and those who are not would demand a high price in concessions local and personal, and even then could not be blindly led. Our working population being mainly native, and very slightly enfranchised, is not at the present day, and will not be for a long time to come, a party powerful enough to make its support a strength to any leader. Then there remained for the Speculatist and Monopolist Party but one body to whom it could turn with any hope that it would place it in power. This body was the Retrogressive Element in the Bond Party. It was purchased, not by the outlay of capital, nor by offers of place and power to its members, but, much more cheaply for the Monopolist, by the simple expedient of offering to support those Retrogressive measures which without his aid could never have found a place on our Colonial Statute-book.

The Kafir's back and the poor man's enhanced outlay on the necessaries of life pay the Monopolist's bribe.

On the other hand, the Retrogressive Element, once enabled to pass such measures as lay nearest its heart by the co-operation of the Monopolist with his skill and intelligence, is willing to give him a perfectly free hand, and support him in all measures which do not touch its Retrogressive instincts. We thus have the

Retrogressive Party supporting the Monopolist in carrying out measures in which he has no interest or concern, and the Monopolist assisting the Retrogressive Party in setting upon the Statute-book measures which are repugnant to his own common sense and shrewd modern outlook. Taking advantage of that childlike simplicity which is at once the weakness and the greatest charm of the Boer, he leads him whither he would and also whither he would not.

It is from this unnatural marriage that are born those evils under which the Colony groans to-day. It is a marriage which must end in rupture when the Retrogressive Party discover how, instead of a union of affection, they have been led into one of convenience, and that the bridegroom is quite ready to forsake his bride when she has nothing more to give him.

Nevertheless, to-day it is this coalition which is unpicking the progressive enactments of the past, which is enabling the Monopolist Party to carry out unhampered its financial depredations here and in the Northern Territories. It is this coalition which, by giving political power to enormously wealthy individuals, is corroding our public life, till the principle that every man has his price and can be squared, if you can only find his figure, is becoming an established dogma.

Worse than any of those retrogressive measures which the Bondsman, in simplicity and sincerity, desires to see enacted are those measures which he allows others to take, who are neither simple nor sincere.

"BUT ARE THEY NOT ANGLICISING AFRICA?"

But I am aware it may be contended : "Granting what has been stated as being exactly true ; allowing that the Monopolist has filched away the wealth of South Africa ; and granting that his party, by coalescing with the extreme Retrogressive Party, has given it for the time being an unhealthy preponderance ; granting, further, that to retain control over the Colonial Legislature squaring in all its multiple forms has been, and is, a necessity on the part of the Monopolist Party ; granting that this is disastrous to our public and social life— yet is it not worth our while to connive at all these conditions, and to abstain from disturbing them, as long as the Monopolist Party is quietly and persistently moving in a direction which tends to annihilate the independence of two adjoining States, which shall ultimately render the Englishman dominant throughout South Africa? At the cost of whatever evils or injustice, is it not well to see extending northward the territory more or less under 'British rule?"

We are all aware that this is often put forth plainly and in so many words as a reason for abstaining from interference with the Monopolist Party. It is said frequently, "I am for Rhodes, because, whatever he may or may not be, he is slowly but surely undermining the Bond. Rhodes, and he only, will within our lifetime so

manipulate, that the neighbouring Republics shall fall into our
hands, and the English Party
in South Africa be dominant.
And, after all, is not this extension to the northward a very
fine thing for the Colony ? "

To this I would first reply :
Is the undermining and breaking up of the Bond, even if
this should result from the
alliance, worth the continual
passing of such measures as we
shall have in the future to
undo ? Is the breaking up of
the Bond itself wholly to be
desired ? And if it were, is
splitting the Bond worth causing
deep racial unrest and suspicion
where none before existed, be-

tween ourselves and our native
fellow-inhabitants, the labouring class of South Africa, by
the passing of laws which seem
to express an animus towards
them which we do not feel;
and which constitute a course
which, though for the moment
it can work us no practical evil,
may in years to come, when
too late, be the cause of bitter
regret? Is it worth while so
vitiating the streams of our
public life that we have to look
back with regret and almost
incredulity at the nature of our
public life in years gone by,
feeling its tone something almost too high ever to have
existed in South Africa? Is

all this worth paying, even if we *are* undermining the Bond ?

I, for one, hold strongly that it is not. I do not wish to see the Bond broken.

What I wish to see is the Bond holding its own manfully on all subjects, social and political, and exercising that influence upon the Legislature and public life of this colony which is proportionate to its numbers and intelligence; thereby preventing legislation from taking a course which might in any respect be unjust, or opposed to the benefit of an important and respected section of the community.

Is the forced annexation of

the neighbouring States worth the price we are paying for it? If it be true, which I question, that the union of the South African States can only be attained by keeping at the head of affairs the Monopolist Party, is it worth keeping them there?

I, for one, assert emphatically that it is not. I believe the confederation of the South African States to be a desirable consummation; and I believe further that it is one which will inevitably take place sooner or later. Confederation *now* might have its advantages, and it would have its disadvantages; but no confederation, however much we desire it, would pay us for the internal disintegration we are producing within our own State, through the support of the Monopolist Party. When confederation does take place I believe it will be desirable that it should take place, not as the result of skilful manipulations analogous to those by which one shrewd speculator out-speculates another, but through the gradual growth of a consciousness in the people of South Africa that their interests are one, and that in union lies their strength. Such a confederacy will, I believe, be as healthful, as strong, as beneficent as a union brought about by sleight - of - hand and dissimulation will be unstable and pernicious.

Is it worth the Cost?

Further, and finally : Is it worth while for us, as Cape Colonists, to submit to the dominion of the Monopolist, with all that pertains to it, simply because we believe that that party, in annexing and apportioning the lands north of the Transvaal and the Cape Colony, is thereby extending the territories under the British flag ?

I, for one, have not only a cordial affection for my own nation, but also for British rule. I believe that, with all its faults, it is often a beneficent and a generous rule ; and were it possible to annex to-morrow, without injustice to others, or heavy moral and social loss to ourselves, the whole of Africa, from the Straits of Gibraltar and the Isthmus of Suez to the Cape Colony, and place it under the English rule, I, for one, should cordially welcome that possibility.

But a nation, like an individual, may pay too dearly for desirable objects. It is highly probable that Naboth's vine-yard, lying as it did contiguous to the domains of Ahab, formed an exceedingly desirable adjunct to that property. The mistake in Jezebel's calculation lay in the fact that the price ultimately to be paid for the annexation somewhat exceeded the value of the land.

I hold, much as I desire to see the extension of the British Empire, that the Colony is in this case paying too dearly for this extension. I hold that no possible accretion of *kudos* and racial gratification can ever repay us for the heavy price in the demoralisation of our institutions, and the retrogression in our legislation, which the Cape Colony is paying to support the Monopolist Group, and enable it to undertake its annexations.

Further, leaving this point of view for a moment, and taking the lower and purely monetary standpoint, let us see what the Colony really has to gain commercially by these annexations south of the Zambesi.

It appears to me there is a good deal of misunderstanding upon this point. I cannot see, from this lower standpoint— nor have I ever yet met a man who could explain to me how he saw—that the taking over of Mashonaland and Matabeleland by the Chartered Company would increase the wealth of the men and women of the Cape Colony. It appears to me more than probable, when we study the map, and other conditions of the problem, that the opening up of these territories, so far from increasing the wealth and influence of the Cape Colony, will ultimately subtract from both. If Rhodesia and the country north of the Transvaal should become populated and important, I cannot for a moment conceive that they will still continue to draw up their supplies from the very toe of South Africa ; that new routes will not be formed, along which trade will make its way to Central and Eastern South Africa, without coming into contact with the extreme south of the Continent.

Further, we as Cape Colonists have *now* more land than we require; our need is for men, and I do not see how the annexation of the Chartered Company tends to draw them into the Cape Colony. I take it that, however wire-pullings may avail for a few years, ultimately the traffic both in passengers and in goods to East and Central South Africa will find the shortest and cheapest routes, which will not be through the Cape Colony; and the Cape Colony, denuded to a large extent of its trade and its importance in South Africa, will have to depend solely upon its internal resources, which, abundant though they be, are now allowed to lie undeveloped, while the people's eyes follow this northern will-o'-the wisp.

But it may be said, and said very truly : " Granting that the Cape Colony does not gain either directly or indirectly through the possession of Rhodesia by the Chartered Company, and even that it loses heavily in the material sense, there is yet no reason, from the broadest humanitarian standpoint, why it should not support the movement."

Now, I fully allow that it may be right and desirable that a portion of a people should sacrifice itself for the benefit of the whole, or that a whole nation should sacrifice itself for the benefit of humanity at large. That this has not yet been done in the history of the world by no means proves that it is undesirable or may not yet be done. But what I most strongly hold is that in this instance sacrifice on the part of the Cape Colony of its internal interests, social and material, if undertaken to enable the Chartered Company to obtain possession of the territories north of the Transvaal, will be sacrifice thrown away.

I know that it will be said, " But think of the terrible contingency had the Boers entered that country and started a new republic there ! "

CHARTERED VERSUS BOER RULE.

I believe *I* shall not be suspected of unreasonable advocacy of Boer rule ; but I do contend that South Africa as a whole, and the English-speaking world at large, would have lost less by the civilisation of these countries under the auspices of the Boer flag than under that of the Chartered Company. Boer rule has its evils ; the Boer is seldom just and considerate to the aborigines of a country which he annexes (though, as a rule, I do not know whether they tend to disappear faster under his rule than under that of other white men) ; but as far as the European is concerned, the rule in a Boer republic is, in most respects, healthy and natural. The Cape Colonist or foreigner from Europe has never been refused admittance to these republics ; and if in the Transvaal the civic franchise has been somewhat injudiciously withheld from certain newcomers, they possess every other privilege and right. As time passes the little racial line between English colonists and their forerunners will pass away throughout South Africa ; the English language will be universally used by all cultured persons ; English manners and customs will prevail (Pretoria is to-day more English than Cape Town !) ; and in the long run, which in this case will only be a run of thirty or forty years, it will make no difference whether any part of this country was first civilised under the flag of the Boer or the Englishman. The incoming streams of English-speaking men and women will slowly but continuously mingle themselves with the body of earlier settlers, and in forty years' time, whether we wish it or do not, there will be no Boer or Englishman as such in South Africa—only the great South African people, speaking the English tongue, following English precedents, and as closely united to England as Australia or Canada.

This process of amalgamation and growth was in progress long before the European speculator arrived among us, and it will go on were the Fates to remove him from us to-morrow.

Had Dutch Voortrekkers taken possession of the regions between the Zambesi and Transvaal there would not, on the whole, have been greater loss of native life, nor more perfidy in dealing with them, than under the Chartered Company ; and one gigantic evil which is now fixing itself upon those territories would not have come into existence. The Boer tradition, like that of the genuine English settler all over the world, has been this : that, in the new lands they inhabited, the soil and the valuable productions of the land should be apportioned fairly among the men who came personally to dwell and labour on it with their wives and families. Rare minerals have not even as a rule been regarded as the property of the individuals in whose lands they were found, but they have been regarded as the property of the community, to any member of which it was open to obtain a share in that property if he were willing to expend his own labour upon it. In States founded in this manner the land and its wealth tended to be distributed with tolerable equality throughout the community. *This will never be in Rhodesia.* By the time the mass of men from the Colony or Europe enter the country they will find everything of value—mines, fertile lands, town properties—all in the hands of a small knot of men headed by the leaders of the Chartered

Company, consisting in part of persons who have never seen South Africa, such as the Duke of Fife and others.

The great evil is not that these men possess the country as shareholders and directors in the Chartered Company, nor that they retain the right to levy a tribute of 50 per cent. on all precious stones and minerals found in the entire territory, and that for many years to come they will hold extensive control over the whole government of the country; but, what is immeasurably more disastrous, before the country can be peopled by the ordinary colonist a small knot of men (not the body of shareholders as a whole, but that small body in whose interest the Chartered Company was formed, and for whose benefit it is worked) will, either in their own persons or by means of their emissaries, have gone over the whole land, and whatever of real value these lands contain will be their private property. If the Chartered Company were in ten or fifteen years' time, or much sooner, to explode, and as a company to loosen its control over the land and people, it would yet be found that the whole real wealth of the country was appropriated and in the hands of a few private individuals forming syndicates and trusts.

The worst social diseases which afflict the old countries of Europe will make their appearance full grown in this virgin African land at the outset of its career. That unequal division of wealth, which bestows vast riches upon some individuals while the majority of the community are in abject poverty, is, in those old countries, the outcome of institutions which are the growth of centuries, and it is often softened by traditions binding the owners of wealth to the land itself, and those who labour on it. In these new territories no traditions will bind the owner to the land and soften his relations with the people ; the financial possessors of the wealth of the country will exhibit on a colossal scale the worst evils of absentee ownership, or the possession of a country by men who regard land and people merely as a means for acquiring wealth.

The political life in these territories will be diseased. Even in the Cape to-day we have seen how disastrous are the effects of gigantic wealth held in a young country by a few individuals. There may be no deliberate intention to bribe, but the mere possession of wealth

which is enormous in compari-
son to the wealth of the whole
community (if the possessors be
not singularly large and impersonal in their aims, and if they
interest themselves at all in
politics) throws into their hands
a power of conferring benefits
or inflicting evils which will
inevitably lead to an undue
subjection to their will ; to the
vitiation of representative institutions, and the destruction of
independent public life.

The colonist and the stranger
from Europe will arrive and
settle in these territories, but
they will discover that its town-
ships, its valuable mines, its
richest lands have already been

taken possession of. They will find it a cake from which all the plums have been carefully extracted, or like a body when the vultures have visited it, leaving nothing but bare bones.

Is it for colonisation carried out on such lines as *these* that the Cape Colony is to be asked to sacrifice its internal political and social welfare? Is it to aid and abet a handful of men in gaining this disastrous control over South Africa and its resources that the Cape Colony is to obliterate itself? Is it to submit to any use which may be made of it, so it only affords a stepping-stone, and gives prestige in Europe by allowing its public appointments to be held by them?

I think not.

CHARTERED VERSUS FOREIGN RULE.

We all know what a bugbear to some even perfectly sincere minds is the conception of the possibility of Boer, Portuguese, German, or French occupation of African territories, and we all know what use is frequently made of this bugbear by those interested in annexations. But I think no practical man who carefully examines the question can really think that the Cape Colonists as such have anything to fear from the annexations of other European Powers in Africa. And I would go further. I would say—If all English colonisation had been, or were in the future to be, carried out along the lines and according to the methods of the Chartered Company, that I cannot see wherein South Africa would gain by aiding and abetting such a form of colonisation over that inaugurated by other European nations. Colonisation by the British people is not the same thing as colonisation under the Chartered Company. The first is supposed to have as its object the development of the people it takes under its rule, and the

planting of a free and untram-
melled branch of the Anglo-
Saxon race upon the land; the
aim of the Chartered Company
is to make wealth out of land
and people.

But last of all, it may be
said (and this criticism appears
to me profoundly just) : " It is
very well to blame the Monopolist, with his ready brains and
his quick wit, for the uses which
he is making of South Africa;
it is very well to blame the
Retrogressive Party for playing
into his hands, and making
possible his monopolies and
increasing acquisitions, making
him a permanent institution in
the land, which the South

Africa of the future may hope-
lessly endeavour to rid herself
of ; it is very well to blame the
Monopolist and Retrogressionist
—but how did they gain, and
how do they maintain, this
absolute domination over the
land ?   Do *they* comprise within
themselves all the intelligence,
all the determination of South
Africa ?   Are they our only
political units ? "

I can but say in reply, I
believe it is not just to throw
the whole blame of our position either upon the Monopolist
or the Retrogressionist. The
Monopolist is simply the acute
business man who has been
enabled to carry out his plans

75

successfully and on a colossal scale, owing to the possession of tact and foresight, and, perhaps, unusual disregard of collateral issues. The high intellectual capacity shown by many of these men compels admiration and awakens our sympathy; and we can only regret that abilities which in some cases amount to genius should not be employed in a direction more productive of good to humanity. The Monopolist of genius is often like a great body of waters expending itself in causing inundations where it might produce fertility.

For the Retrogressionist there is yet more unlimited excuse.

He has been somewhat hardly dealt with in the past. That he should desire to make his influence felt when at last the opportunity offers itself, and that he should use his power without full consideration for the rights of others, is not un-natural. He alone among South Africans has, during the last years, shown a capacity for standing resolutely by his principles ; and we can only feel regret that so much integrity and manly determination is not expended on our side, but against us.

But there are two other sections of our population upon whom it appears to me unlimited blame rests, and for whom it is difficult to see an excuse.

Two Other Culprits.

Firstly. There is that section of the general public which, knowing that we are governed by representative institutions, and that every citizen, however humble, is more or less responsible for the well-being of the State, yet regards public affairs with apathy; and, absorbed in personal interests, is absolutely ungrateful of its citizens' duties.

Secondly (and for this section it appears to me that no reprobation can be too strong). We have a party of men throughout South Africa, by education and natural bias, Liberals ; by public profession, Progressives ; men who on their own showing see clearly the evils of Retrogressive and Monopolist principles, and who constitute part of our so-called Progressive Party. These men, in spite of their profession, are continually found, as public men and leaders, using the subtlest methods of the Monopolist, coquetting with any and every party which appears likely to aid them to office and power. Without the genius of the Monopolist, they sink to his opportunism for the attainment of the smallest ends ; as private individuals they oppose such progressive measures which would entail inconvenience upon themselves, personally or locally, and connive at certain retrogressive measures when doing so confers benefit upon themselves, without the true Retrogressive's excuse of earnest conviction. It is these men, whether politicians, progressive farmers, or enlightened commercial men, to whom we should naturally look for deliverance from the evils which oppress the Colony; yet it is exactly these men who in some instances have made possible the despotism of the Monopolist, and the triumph of the

Retrogressionist, by their complete absorption in their own small aims, and their wilful disregard of impersonal obligations. The Monopolist may be organically incapacitated for seeing further; the Retrogressionist, in spite of his sincerity, cannot see further; the so-called Progressive sees further, but refuses to act at any cost to himself. Such men are the bane of the country.

There is, however, yet another section of our community distinct from all those we have noticed. It is to this section, I think, that we must look to inaugurate a truly Progressive movement in Colonial affairs.

And this brings us back to the question with which we started : How is the Retro-gressive Movement in the Cape Colony to be Stayed?

PART II.

PART II.

How is the Retrogressive Movement to be Stayed?

To this question the reply seems obvious : That in a country with representative institutions Retrogressive legislation must be prevented, if prevented at all, by the intervention of such Progressive Elements as exist within the community itself.

Is there a Progressive Factor?

But when we look at the Cape Colony at the present day, the doubt at first forces itself upon us whether there is a Progressive Element at all. Would this unbroken spell of Retrogressive legislation and political flaccidity be possible were really Progressive Elements existent in the country?

In times past there was such an element. Small but united, there was a Progressive Party of which no advanced European people need have been ashamed. From the days of Pringle and Fairbairn to the days of Sir George Grey and Saul Solomon, not only was South Africa not wanting in liberal and advanced individuals, but these individuals had their influential following. It was by these men and their party that our most advanced institutions were created, our comparatively broad basis of enfranchisement instituted, our most beneficent educational establishments, native and otherwise, founded, and the recognition on our Statute-book of the fact that to all men, irrespective of race and colour, the law should deal out an even-handed justice—this and much more was the work of these men.

When to-day we see how steadily we are undoing this work, and legislating in opposition to it, and how entirely opposed to the Progressive spirit of the past is that which guides our public councils to-day, the suggestion will force itself upon us: " Is not the Progressive Element dying or dead among us?"

For years past Retrogressive measure after Retrogressive measure has stained our Statute-book; undesirable commercial contracts have been entered into, subjecting public interests to personal gains; the name and prestige of the Cape Colony have been used for the attainment of extra-colonial ends in a manner we do not desire— yet we have remained passive. In town or village no public meetings have been called to protest against these courses of action. In no case have even the smallest knots of men been found banded together to defend the country against these changes. If we except the recent protest against the bread and meat tax and against the appointment of one of the Monopolist Party to the highest function of the State, the country has remained in a condition of deadly passivity and almost comatose inertia.

On the surface I allow it

appears that there is no progressive element in South Africa,
but I believe this appearance is
not a reality.

I believe that in every town,
and in every district and village,
will be found (though not in-
variably among its most important or wealthy members) a
certain body of men and women,
from the bank clerk to the
clergyman, from the shop assis-
tant to the small tradesman,
from the schoolmaster or
mistress to the enterprising
young farmer, Dutch or English,
from the working man to the
wholesale merchant, who are as
essentially advanced in their
view as any body of men or

women in any country : persons wholly unaffected by the disease which seems eating the core of our national life—that fevered desire to grow wealthy without labour, as individuals by reckless speculation, and as a nation by annexations.

And if it be asked how, if this Progressive Element exists among us, it has become so completely inoperative, my reply is simply—*Because it lacks organisation.*

At the time of the Restoration there were not fewer advanced and progressive Republicans in England than there had been in the lifetime of Oliver Cromwell. They had not died nor emigrated at the accession of Charles the Second ; they were still there, holding their views with the same strength and with perhaps an added bitterness, but as a power in the land they were annihilated. They had lost their leader ; they had lost their organisation ; and the extreme Retrogressive Party had attained to both of these. That mass of persons, indifferent to reforms and public interests, which is found in every country, and which sides with each dominant party because it has the power of conferring benefits and inflicting injuries, went over to the Royalists as it had before gone over to the Republicans. The Democratic Party for years was inoperative in England, but it was not dead, only disorganised ; it came to life again, more democratic than ever.

So, looking nearer home, there were not, eleven years ago, fewer non-progressive and reactionary persons in the Colony than at the present day : there were probably more.

The men who have raised the franchise, who have taxed the necessaries of life, who have crushed all endeavours to contend with scab, who session by session attempt to pass a Flogging Bill which would disgrace a semi-barbarous people, have not sprung into existence to-day; they were here, holding their views if possible more ardently than to-day, but they were powerless; they could not even materially impede Progressive legislation, because they were unorganised.

This position is ours to-day. Exactly as the Anti-Progressive individual sat on his farm, unable to give expression to his views, because he sat alone, and had no means of communicating with his like-thinking and like-feeling fellows, so to-day the Progressive men and women stand alone in this country; they are not aware of their own numbers ; they are not aware of the intensity of common conviction which would bind them into a solid body were they once in touch.

The organisation of these now scattered and isolated units into one united whole is, I believe, the one and only means of staying the Retrogressive Movement in this country. And the great practical question before us now is—How is this to be done?

I allow that I see great difficulties in the way.

Wanted : a Leader.

One of the first and most essential conditions for organising a party is the possession of a leader ; we will not say of an Oliver Cromwell, but at least of a progressive J. H. Hofmeyr ; of a man profoundly in sympathy with the movement, with a gift for organisation, and a willingness to sink his own personal interests to a large extent in that of his work. It is such a man the Progressive Element in this country looks for. We have not found him yet. We have more than one public man of undoubted ability ; and we have at least one man who carries with him the confidence and affection of every Progressive in the country ; but either from some peculiarity of nature, from absence of leisure, or other circumstances, none of these men stand forward, devoting time and energy to the formation of such a party throughout the country. We have not a man to whom the Progressive can turn and say : "Organise and lead us ; we will follow!" The necessity is therefore imposed upon us of organising ourselves. Nor do I know that this is wholly a calamity.

The most vital and world-wide movements of the present day, such as those of labour and woman, have not been organised or led by one commanding intellect. They have sprung up spontaneously, as it were, in a thousand centres, and then slowly interorganised. It is a healthy indication of a profound necessity when men at independent centres organise themselves, guided by a common impulse without any coercing leadership.

This is exactly what we see taking place in the Colony to-day. The imposition of the bread and meat tax and the appointment of Sir Hercules Robinson have drawn together small knots of Progressive men to protest against these things ; and in such towns as Port Elizabeth and in Cape Town, under the presidency of Mr. J. Rose-Innes, powerful Progressive Associations have been started.

And the time is, I believe, now ripe for drawing together all the scattered Progressive Elements of the country, and uniting them as a wide and non-parochial whole. One, and not the least, of the great advantages of such union would be its tendency to prevent the growth in the Progressive Party of that spirit of localism which seems to rest as an incubus upon all Colonial endeavours, and which would be entirely at variance with the true spirit of a Progressive Organisation.

To place at the head of the united branches no man could be found more admirably suited than Mr. J. Rose-Innes, the president of the South African Political Association of Cape Town, if he were found willing to accept the post.

FORM ASSOCIATIONS.

I think as a first and practical step towards this larger union it would be desirable that wherever possible, in towns or districts, a few progressive men should join together and form Progressive Associations, however small in size, analogous to those now existing in Port Elizabeth and Cape Town. It would then be desirable that these bodies should enter into communication with each other, and draw up a body of principles broad enough to make it possible for every really progressive individual to subscribe to them, and distinct enough to make it quite impossible for any thoroughly non-progressive person to enter the organisation. These principles, I think, should be made the basis of all future organisation.

As a second step, I think it would be advisable that, if possible, a delegate should be appointed to visit each town and village in the Colony to attempt to inaugurate a branch of our organisation, however small, in that place. The advantage of this course is obvious. It is often difficult for any individual in a small Colonial town to rise up and inaugurate a movement of any kind, unless he chance to be of exceptional importance, monetarily or otherwise, in the place. In many towns there may be even a large number of individuals, progressive at heart, who would join such an organisation, and who would labour for it vigorously and be able to extend its growth, who yet might not feel themselves in a position to rise up and take the initiative in instating it.

It may be objected that, in

places where the branch would at first consist of only a dozen individuals, it would be useless, and serve only to show the barrenness of the land !

But, firstly, while an organisation consisting of a dozen isolated individuals in some town or village might be of small importance in itself, connected as it would ultimately be with the organisations in larger towns throughout the country, its strength would be largely increased ; and it would form the germ of what might in time become an extensive growth. It is exactly that we may not lose these driblets of progressive thought and feeling all over the Colony that I would advocate the endeavour to start such small branch organisations.

If further it be asked, What the principles are which are broad enough to unite all the Progressive Elements in the country? I think an answer will not be very difficult.

There are one or two principles subscription to which will make a man a Liberal and Progressive in any country in the world. Their practical application will vary infinitely according to the conditions of the Society in which they are applied ; but they are as simple as universal.

The fundamental principle [1] upon which Progressive Liberalism all the world over is based, whether consciously or unconsciously, and to which it must finally return if it would justify its varying forms of practical action, is the axiom, however variously worded, which asserts that the mental and physical welfare and happiness of hu-

[1] There is also that ancient categorical imperative which has lain behind the Liberalism of all religious natures from the days of Buddha and Confucius to that of Jesus and the Socialistic movement of to-day—" Do ye unto others as ye would they should do unto you "—and which, perhaps, after all, is the most satisfactory statement of the fundamental principle of Liberalism yet formulated.

manity as a whole is the end
of all wisely directed human
effort, whether of individuals
or nations ; that one of the
main aims of all government
must be the defence of its
weaker members from the depredations of the stronger, and
that no course of action which
bases the welfare of sections of
the community on the sufferings
and loss of other sections is
justifiable.

Analysis shows that it is
upon this wide principle, however worded, that all forms of
Modern Liberalism are ultimately based. It is by their
more or less complete harmony
with it that the thoroughness

of their Liberalism may be tested. Nevertheless, it is perhaps too wide a principle on which to base directly a practical organisation intended for the many ; more especially in a country where some men's conceptions with regard to Liberal Progressivism are somewhat indefinite—a prominent public man having declared that he considered himself a Progressive because he voted for the construction of railways which would be for his own pecuniary benefit.

THREE TEST QUESTIONS.

In the Cape Colony, and for such an Association as we propose, there are, I think, three subjects, a man's attitude with regard to which would amply suffice to show his adherence or otherwise to this fundamental principle underlying all Liberalism ; and which, I think, would be adequate as a test of the fitness of any individual for membership in a Progressive Organisation.

The first of these is the Labour Question ; the question of the relation between the propertied, and therefore powerful, class, and the less propertied, and therefore weaker, class.

In South Africa this question assumes gigantic importance, including as it does almost the whole of what is popularly termed the Native Question ; that question being indeed only the Labour Question of Europe complicated by a difference of race and colour between the employing and propertied, and the employed and poorer classes.

There are two attitudes with regard to the treatment of this Native Labouring Class : the one held by the Retrogressive Party in this country regards the Native as only to be tolerated in consideration of the amount of manual labour which can be extracted from him ; and desires to obtain the largest amount of labour at the cheapest rate possible ; and rigidly resists all endeavours to put him on an equality with the white man in the eye of the law. The other attitude, which I hold must inevitably be that of every truly progressive individual in this country, is that which regards the Native, though an alien in race and colour and differing fundamentally from ourselves in many respects, yet as an individual to whom we are under certain obligations : it forces on us the conviction that our superior intelligence and culture render it obligatory upon us to consider his welfare ; and to carry out such measures, not as shall make him merely more useful to ourselves, but such as shall tend also to raise him in the scale of existence, and bind him to ourselves in a kindlier fellowship.

As a man takes one or other of these attitudes I believe he will find himself in accord, not merely with the Progressive Element in this country, but with the really advanced and Progressive Movement all the world over. In fact, I go so far as to think that the mere subscription to the latter mode of regarding the Labour and Native question would constitute an adequate test in this country as to a man's attitude on all other matters social and political.

The second subject is that of Taxation.

The Retrogressive holds, all the world over, that taxation may be levied for the benefit of the few. The Progressive attitude is that which holds that taxation should fall upon the luxuries rather than upon the necessaries of life ; that it should not press more heavily upon the poor than upon the wealthy ; and that the principle of protection, worked so as to increase the wealth of certain sections of the community at the expense of others, is at all points to be fought.

The third subject upon which I believe the views of every advanced Progressive must and will coincide is that of enfranchisement.

No man who does not hold that as a State develops its electoral basis should be extended to obviate the possibility of the claims of the unrepresented classes being ignored, and their welfare subordinated to that of represented, though smaller classes, and who does not hold that Parliamentary representation should increasingly tend to represent individuals rather than property, can find himself in harmony with the principles of any real Progressive Organisation.

It may be said that these

principles are too vague ; that the articles to which a man would have to subscribe before joining such an organisation should be more detailed.

But I think a little consideration will show that upon all the practical questions which have been brought before our Colonial Legislature during the last few years, subscription to these three principles of action would have determined a man's attitude. The Labour Tax, Haarhoff's Curfew Bell, the Bread and Meat Tax, the Strop Bill, the Scab Act, &c.—on all these a man's position will be certainly and at once determined by the fact of his being willing to subscribe to these three principles. A more detailed test for fitness of membership in the organisation would, I think, be superfluous.

But it may, on the other hand, be objected that these tests would be too stringent ; that certain men would be found quite willing to join a so-called Progressive and anti-Bond Party who at the same time might not be willing to subscribe to one or all these tests.

Now to these I would unhesitatingly answer : That such men are not wanted in our organisation ; men who, while holding retrogressive views on the most

important social questions, but
prompted by an unworthy
racial prejudice, would attempt
to join or use the organisation
for racial purposes, hoping to
oppose or weaken the party
behind the Bond, are precisely
that class of persons we should
seek to exclude from our organisation. They would weaken
us, and defeat that very end
for which the organisation was
formed. It must of necessity
be a first principle of such an
association as we wish to see
started that no racial or class
distinction of any kind should
concern it, or be allowed to
weigh with us. We should re-
joice as cordially to welcome

and support the Dutchmen as the Englishmen; the new-comer as the old inhabitant of the country; the man as the woman; the wealthy as the in-digent. Our sole requirement from any individual wishing to join us, or seeking our support, should be, Does he share our principles? If he does, he is one of us; if he does not, though he should call himself a Progressive leader, and though he should be seven times over an Englishman, he is not of us.

If it be further suggested that, by pursuing this course, we should alienate large bodies of persons who would otherwise append themselves to us, and

who might ultimately so swell
our numbers as to make us the
dominant party in the State, I
would frankly reply that no
mere increase of bulk could
compensate us for degeneracy
in fibre, and that we do not
desire the adhesion of such
individuals to our party. Our
strength will not, and cannot,
rest upon mere numbers. It
must lie in the enthusiasm, in
the superior intelligence, in the
unwavering adhesion to impersonal aims, and in the close-knit
union of our members.

The Progressive Element in
this country is, and must be for
many years to come, necessarily
in a minority, exactly as the

extreme Non-Progressive Element is in a minority. Between us lies the large inert body of politicians and private persons, indifferent to any aims but those of personal success, and the person of sincere but very mixed convictions. This body follows to-day the Non-Progressive Party, because it is the only vigorous and unbending political organisation existent in the country. If to-morrow there were in the field a small but vigorous Progressive Party, well organised, and not willing to capitulate upon any terms, this inert, self-seeking body might also find it useful to serve us ; it might even ultimately give to us the appearance of being the majority in the State, exactly as it to-day does to the Retrogressive Party. But as from the day on which the extreme Retrogressive Party shall resign its principles, and with a feeble opportunism shall receive into its own organisation this inert mass, the day of its dissolution and disappearance from Governmental control will have arrived; so also with the Progressive Party. From the day on which it sacrifices its position as the enlightened leading minority, and modifies its principles for the purpose of making them acceptable to the indifferent majority in the country, from that moment it will have nullified the aim with which it was started, and all its powers of accomplishment.

I think we cannot too strongly impress upon, and hold up before ourselves, the fact that such a Progressive Party as we hope to see in this country can only maintain its power by firm adhesion to its own principles, and not by any dependence on numbers.

If it be questioned how, in default of large numbers, we expect to exert influence and make our principles operative in the country, I would reply, that for many years our primary practical aim must be the attempt to educate public opinion up to our own standpoint.

Our means for accomplishing this would, it appears to me, be mainly three.

Firstly. We shall form a centre, however small, in every town or village from which, by the exercise of personal influence, the view of life which the organisation represents would tend to spread, and however small the branch might be, it would keep before the eye of the public the fact that such a view did exist.

Secondly. We should use the Press.

USE THE PRESS.

The great strength of such a party as the Progressive Party of South Africa must be would lie in the superior intellectual enlightenment of its members. I take it that it is not likely any large body of men will join such an organisation who have not the intelligence and culture which would enable them to think somewhat deeply upon social matters. I believe we should largely represent the thinking element in the community, whether our members were drawn from the labouring or wealthier class.

Such a body, with no narrow

personal ends to seek, will naturally desire the largest publicity for its views, and will also have the power of expressing them. Of such a party the main weapon is the Press. It will find one of its chief duties for many years in constantly raising and animating public discussion upon all questions, social and political, as they arise, and in unflinchingly enunciating its own views, and calling forth the enunciation of those of others—a function of paramount importance in a country where men often, even in private conversation, fear to speak above their breath, lest a bird of the air should carry it.

We shall make rich use of all the public journals in the country. But if the Progressive Party is to become a power which shall make itself felt, I believe its most powerful weapon must be the possession of a journal devoted entirely to its principles.

With a very few exceptions there is a generous attitude maintained in Colonial papers, and their columns are freely open to correspondents. We are rich in able and liberal editors, and our Press in many ways is in advance of other Colonial institutions. But the fact, which all who have been behind the scenes of Press life in this country are aware of (and of which the public appears *not* to be aware !), is that no editor, however able and advanced, has, as a rule, an absolute control over his paper. In the vast majority of cases in the Colony, as in England, the newspaper is a property held by a larger or smaller number of shareholders ; it is finally theirs, and should the editor himself be a large shareholder, he has yet not always an independent and free hand. A certain amount of liberty is granted him, and he may imagine himself independent ; but when crucial commercial or political questions arise, at the very moment when he would most desire to stand firm, and unqualifiedly to express his own views, those persons with whom the real and ultimate control rests may step in ; and whether simply fearing that the commercial value of the paper may decline if an unpopular course be persisted in ; or, immeasurably worse still, actuated by personal motives, may desire to use the paper for their own commercial or political benefit —then he may be required to alter his tone or remain silent.

No knowledge of the high principle and personal integrity of an editor can give the public assurance that personal influences may not be compelling him to modify his course. He is often but an able and highly accredited agent ; and he may, under these circumstances, conscientiously feel that he is not justified in pursuing a course which would result in commercial loss to those whose property he manages. He may throw up his control (which is often impossible), or he must remain silent. Men who would be incorruptible before any conceivable species of bribe might, nay, almost must, be amenable to this pressure of circumstances and obligations.

If a paper is to represent undeviatingly and sincerely a

certain body of opinions, it is absolutely necessary either that it should be completely under the control of one man who is wholly devoted to the body of principles to be maintained, or it must be the property of an organisation representing these principles. Even in this case, were the shares held by members of the organisation, it would be necessary for them to safeguard themselves from the possibility of individual shareholders being induced to sell their shares to the persons, or emissaries of the persons, who would be interested in vitiating the standpoint of the paper.

It would be necessary to make

it impossible for any shareholder to dispose of a share
without the consent of either
the Executive Committee of
the Organisation, or of all other
shareholders, and for any individual shareholder to possess
more than a certain limited
number of shares. It would
then be open only to the personal corruption of individual
shareholders,—a contingency
against which no foresight or
caution can avail, but of which
there would be little danger were
the original shareholders carefully selected.

A paper safeguarded through
one or other of these conditions
is, I believe, absolutely essential

to the real success of a Progressive Organisation. Such a paper the Progressive Element in South Africa possessed when Saul Solomon had absolute control of the *Cape Argus;* and such a paper must yet be the rallying point of the Progressive Party in this country.

The third method by which the association could impress itself upon the country would be by the share it would take in political life.

INFLUENCE POLITICIANS !

If it be questioned how, if our numbers be too small to return a majority to the Legislative Councils and to place our men in office, we propose to influence political life, I would reply, that we neither expect nor, for many years to come, desire to see a Ministry formed of our own men.

The truly Progressive Element in this country is to-day in a minority, of about the same numerical strength as the extreme Retrogressive Party; neither of these parties to-day is strong enough to put into office and to support, even for a time, a Ministry of its own, consistently carrying out its views. Neither of them could command so completely the Intermediate or Colourless Party as to give it a working majority, save by bartering away the very principles, the support of which formed the sole cause of its existence.

The extreme Retrogressive Party in this country has maintained its power, as all conscientious minorities must do, by not seeking to grasp in its hands the ostensible reins of Government, and by its leaders being willing to forego the sweets of office for the sake of effectively impressing the views of the party upon successive Ministries.

By such a course of action the Irish Party, composing a minority in the Imperial Parliament, has yet for years made itself a power, courted and feared by successive Liberal and Conservative Governments, and has been able to force its views before the public. Had its leaders as individuals thirsted, not for the success of the principles they represented, but merely to attain office in some incoming Government, they would either have had to desert their party, or their party would have been compelled to rest content with the pleasure of saying, "There are Irishmen in the Government," in place of seeing their aims upheld. Had the people of Ireland set before themselves as their main end the seeing of certain of their representatives on the Government benches, they could only have attained it by their representatives ceasing to be Irishmen in everything but name; and the Irish vote would have been annihilated at the very moment of a shallow seeming triumph.

Such would be the fate of the truly Progressive or truly Non-Progressive party in this country, if it should set before itself, as its chief end, the placing of its own men in office.

In a country with representative institutions a minority, unless it uses force or bribery, *cannot* place its men in office, and maintain them there for

even the shortest period, without sacrificing its very existence.
This is trite and obvious, but
we dwell upon it because it
appears often completely over-
looked in the discussion of
political affairs in this country;
and the fatuous conception
seems to prevail that a party
can only affect the country and
the course of legislation if some
person, or persons, who osten-
sibly belong to its organisation,
at whatever cost to its principles,
hold office in the Government
of the day.

The truly Progressive Element in this country will not
contain within itself the large
majority of the inhabitants

for the next five, ten, or perhaps even fifteen years. If the
majority of our inhabitants
stand, in fifteen years' time,
where the majority of the inhabitants of New Zealand stand
to-day, we shall feel that the
richest hopes of the Progressives of this country have been
fulfilled.

The part which the Progressive Association in this country
will have to play, perhaps for
many years, is that of a small,
united party, strong in its intelligence and determination,
and, above all, in the absolutely
unpurchasable nature of its
members. A small but united
body, it would have to be

reckoned with by each successive Ministry as it took office, and, because it could neither be purchased or bent, would be a thorn in the side of every Government intent upon carrying out measures at variance with its views.

If it be asked by what exact means we could make our influence felt by these successive Ministries, I would reply that we should influence them, firstly, by our free and uncompromising discussion in the Colonial and European press of their methods of action and the measures which they introduced. In a country which is rotten with opportunism, and where we have reached a point in which a man dares hardly to give utterance in whispers to his political convictions, and in which hundreds of men and women sit spell-bound, afraid of losing their daily bread if they utter a word in condemnation of existing powers, the fact of persistent and fearless discussion of governmental methods would render the continuance of certain existing lines of action on the part of Government almost impossible. Autocratic Governments have nothing so much to dread as free criticism.

Secondly : Our branches would form centres in every

town and village for the prompt calling of public meetings to protest against undesirable measures. Had such an organisation been in existence recently when the news reached this Colony of an unpopular appointment, instead of a knot of Progressive men in a few Colonial towns having to organise themselves into small bodies for that particular purpose, it would merely have been necessary to send the news to all branches, and within forty-eight hours, in almost every town and village in the Colony, those men who were opposed to the appointment would have met and discussed the matter, and sent forth their protests.

Thirdly: We should influence the political world through our electoral functions.

A Group of Twelve.

I do not doubt that there would be ten or a dozen men in Parliament who would represent our views, some or all of them belonging to our organisation. These men, feeling that they had a considerable body behind them, might more easily be induced to stand firmly, and refuse all offers of office, or local and personal benefits, which could be accepted only at the cost of laying aside their functions of criticism.

At elections we should exert our influence. In every instance we should, if we were true to our principles, throw our weight, small though it might be, into the scale of that man, whether Dutchman or Englishman, whom we could most depend upon to act in accordance with our principles or do least violence to them. Where we could not possibly return a member of our own we could, by throwing our weight in the scale of the man most desirable or least objectionable, turn many elections. If, as an organisation, we stood firm to our convictions, we should frequently have the casting vote.

I think it will be necessary for us to set clearly before ourselves from the very start the fact that we have not organised ourselves to support any given body of politicians, but to see our policy enforced; that we have nailed to our mast-head, not the names of individuals, but a declaration of our principles. While a man acts in accordance with these, he is one of us; when he does not, then he ceases to be of us. We could as little have supported the recent Ministry under Mr. Rhodes, because three of the ablest and most liberal men of the country bore office in it, as we could the present Ministry. The bitterest wrong which leaders can inflict upon their crew is when they take service on the enemy's ship, and prevent their fellows from attacking it, for fear of wounding them. Under such circumstances there is nothing to be done but to fire, regardless whether you bring down your own absconded leaders or the enemy; and this, even though they may have been partly actuated by a desire to impede the enemy's sailing powers when they took service.

As Progressives, we should not be moved an inch out of

our path by the fact that any man calls himself an Oppositionist, or is the member of any existing Government. We should endeavour to support or oppose any man or Ministry with strict impartiality, exactly as it opposed or supported the principles we represent. As long as a man, in any single instance, supported them, did he call himself Bondsman or Retrogressive, he should have our steadfast approval.

That captious criticism, and disingenuous judgment, which would condemn any measure brought in or supported by a member of an opposing political faction, and which is almost inevitable where men have turned politics into a game, and are playing to make points, should be wholly foreign to the spirit of such an organisation as our own, whose chief end should be the passing of those measures we believe beneficial, and not the seeing of those men who call themselves our representatives for the moment captains in the political game.

Were such an organisation as I have suggested formed which would draw into itself the scattered Progressive Elements throughout the whole country, despising none ; and which should seek to draw its strength, not from numbers, but from the

determination and the impersonal
aims of its members ; which
should endeavour to influence
political life without throwing
itself into the whirlpool of
political ambitions ; and which
should stand outside, consistently fighting for its own
principles—such an organisation, though including perhaps
at first not many noted political
names, but formed of the people
and for the people, would, I
believe, slowly and surely grow.
For the first two years our
occupation would be mainly
that of self-organisation, and
the education of public feeling.
I believe that in five years' time
we should be a power in the

land, able to restore the Retrogressive Influences to that healthy and natural position in which they would form a conservative safeguard, preventing the inauguration of measures too far in advance of the social condition of the community. I believe that in fifteen or twenty years' time our aims, which now appear chimerical to a part of the community, will be then but an attempt to give voice to the convictions of the people. And this I believe is worth working and waiting for.

UNWIN BROTHERS, THE GRESHAM PRESS,
WOKING AND LONDON.

Pros ectus o

Works About

AFRICA

AND

AFRICANS.

PUBLISHED BY
T. FISHER UNWIN,
PATERNOSTER SQ.,
LONDON, E.C.

ADAMS, FRANCIS—

THE NEW EGYPT. By Francis Adams.
Large Crown 8vo, 5s.

BROWN, ROBERT—

PELLOW'S ADVENTURES AND SUFFERINGS DURING HIS CAPTIVITY IN MOROCCO.
Edited by Robert Brown, Ph.D. Being Vol. IV. of *The Adventure Series*. (N.B.—*The Adventure Series* consists of 18 volumes, each large crown 8vo, fully illustrated. Volumes 1 to 14 are bound in red cloth, price 5s. each, and volumes 15 to 18 are elegantly bound in cloth extra, gilt, gilt tops, 7s. 6d. each.)

"Full of strange tales and wild adventures."
—THE TIMES.

BURLEIGH, BENNET—

IN PREPARATION.

TWO CAMPAIGNS: Madagascar and
Ashantee, 1895-6. By Bennet Burleigh, War Correspondent to the *Daily Telegraph*. 50 Illustrations. Demy 8vo, 16s.

By way of introduction the author remarks that "Two Campaigns" is the history of recent events in Madagascar and Ashantee. Subjects of general interest, as well as military operations are dealt with. Both have been epoch-making campaigns, so far as the countries named are concerned. By force of arms great political and social changes have been introduced into these lands. Whether the ultimate appeal to the sword was warranted in either case, the reader when furnished with the facts can later on determine for himself. For several reasons "Two Campaigns" are included within one book. I was present in both, and most of that which is written herein, is from personal observation. Madagascar and Ashantee though so widely apart have much in common and much that differs. The columns of the *Daily Telegraph* have contained a great deal of the information gathered in either land during my wanderings. Unfortunately the hurry incident to writing for the daily press is often unsuited to the production of a complete and rounded record. A still more serious drawback than that, however, frequently affects the work. During the stress of war, for good or evil, the inner side of things has sometimes to be left severely alone. As I can now write with a free hand, there is added to my former narrative many things that are new and true and worthy of being made part of the chronicle. I am sanguine enough to believe that all classes will find something to interest them within the pages of " Two Campaigns." '

CLAIRMONTE, E.—

THE AFRICANDER : A Plain Tale of Colonial Life. By E. CLAIRMONTE. Illustrated. Crown 8vo, cloth, 6s.

The author's experiences from 1877 to a recent date form the major part of this book. He has endeavoured, *en passant*, to describe the Boer, and to indicate the circumstances which have made him what he is—a strange survival of patriarchal times. The Boer war and the Kaffir wars are also dwelt on, and the customary details concerning sport, adventure, gold and diamond-digging are not wanting."

DRURY, ROBERT—

MADAGASCAR ; or, Robert Drury's Journal during his Fifteen Years Captivity. Edited by Captain S. P. OLIVER. Vol. II. of *The Adventure Series.* Cr. 8vo, cloth, 5s.

THE PALL MALL GAZETTE says :—" It is full of incidents quaintly told. . . The cuts are curious, and the miscellaneous matter is of more than ordinary interest."

IRON, RALPH—

DREAM LIFE AND REAL LIFE. By RALPH IRON (Olive Schreiner). Third Edition. Being Vol. XXXII. of *The Pseudonym Library*. Paper 1s. 6d. Cloth, 2s

JAPP, ALEXANDER HAY—

MASTER MISSIONARIES: Studies in Heroic Pioneer Work. By A. H. JAPP, LL.D. 7th Edition. (Being Vol. III. of *The Lives Worth Living Series of Popular Biographies*.) Illustrated. Crown 8vo, cloth extra, 3s. 6d. 6 vols. in handsome box, 21s. "Master Missionaries" contains ten biographical chapters including "Robert Moffat and South Africa," and "Dr. William Black and Livingstonia."

LLOYD, Rev. EDWIN—

THREE GREAT AFRICAN CHIEFS (Khâmé, Sebelé, and Bathoeng). B the Rev. E. LLOYD (Lond. Mis. Soc.). y2nd Edition, revised and enlarged and brought up to date. 4 portraits. Cr. 8vo, cl., 3s. 6d.

THE CHRISTIAN WORLD says:—"Mr. Lloyd has much that is interesting to tell us of the two chiefs who [accompanied] Khama in this country. His book is pleasant to read."

MAXWELL, J. R.

THE NEGRO QUESTION: or, Hints for the Physical Improvement of the Negro Race. By JOSEPH RENNER MAXWELL, M.A., B.C.L. Crown 8vo, cloth, 6s.

THE DAILY TELEGRAPH says:—"In its fearless grappling with difficult questions and its outspoken hostility to race prejudices, the book is worthy of much praise."

MOFFAT, JOHN SMITH—

THE LIVES OF ROBERT AND MARY MOFFAT. By their son, JOHN SMITH MOFFAT. Tenth Edition. Illust. Demy 8vo, cloth, 7s. 6d.

NEWMAN, Capt. C. L. NORRIS—
MATABELELAND, and How We Got It.
By Capt. CHARLES L. NORRIS NEWMAN.
Large crown 8vo, cloth, with Maps, 7s. 6d.
SOUTH AFRICA says: "There is much that
is entertaining in these reminiscences, and the author's
own interesting personality will also attract South
Africans to purchase his book."

POOLE, STANLEY LANE—
THE BARBARY CORSAIRS. By STAN-
LEY LANE-POOLE. Large crown 8vo,
cloth, 5s. Being vol. xxii of *The Story of
the Nations.*—Also to be had in half Persian,
cloth sides, gilt tops. Price on application.

RAWLINSON, Canon GEORGE—
ANCIENT EGYPT. Being Vol. VII of
The Story of the Nations..

SCHREINER, OLIVE—
DREAMS. By OLIVE SCHREINER ("Ralph
Iron"). 7th Ed. Demy 12mo, cl., 2s. 6d.

SCULLY, W. C.—
KAFIR STORIES. By W. C. SCULLY.
Being Vol. X of *The Autonym Library.*
Paper, 1s. 6d., cloth, 2s.
THE WHITEHALL REVIEW says: "There
is something startlingly fascinating in some of these
tales."

POEMS. By W. C. SCULLY. Fcap. 8vo,
cloth, 4s. 6d.

SEARELLE, L.—
TALES OF THE TRANSVAAL. By
LUSCOMBE SEARELLE. Illustrated by
P. Franzeny, and after Photographs. 8vo
cloth, 2s. 6d.

SIBREE, JAMES—
IN PREPARATION.
MADAGASCAR AND THE MALAGASY. By JAMES SIBREE. Illustrated With Map. Demy 8vo, cloth, 21s.

The Volume consists of the following chapters :— i. From Coast to Capital : Notes of a Journey from Mahanoro to Antananarivo ; ii. Imerina, the Central Province : Its Physical Features and Village Life ; iii. Antananarivo, the Capital ; Its Public Buildings, Memorial and other Churches, and Religious and Charitable Institutions ; iv. The Changing Year in Central Madagascar : Notes on the Climate, Agriculture, Social Customs of the People, and Varied Aspects of the Months ; v. The Crater Lake of Tritriva : Its Physical Features and Legendary History and the Volcanic Regions of the Interior ; vi. Ambatovory, one of our Holiday Resorts in Madagascar ; vii. Malagasy Place-names ; viii. Curious Words and Customs connected with Chieftainship and Royalty among the Malagasy, and Notes on Relics of the Sign and Gesture Language ; ix. Malagasy Folk-Lore and Popular Superstitions ; x. Malagasy Oratory, Ornaments of Speech, Symbolic Actions and Conundrums ; xi. Malagasy Songs, Poetry, Children's Games and Mythical Creatures ; xii. Malagasy Folk-Tales and Fables ; xiii. Divination among the Malagasy ; xv. Decorative Carving on Wood, especially on the Burial Memorials of the Betsileo Malagasy, together with Notes on the Handicrafts of the Malagasy and Native Products : xvi. Odd and Curious Experiences of Life in Madagascar ; xix. The Birds of Madagascar with Notes on their Habits and Habitats and their connection with Native Folk-Lore and Superstition ; xxi. A Quarter-Century of Change and Progress : Antananarivo and Madagascar Twenty-Five Years Ago and Now.

SMITH, *Lieutenant* HARRISON—
THROUGH ABYSSINIA: An Envoy's Ride to the King of Zion. By Lieut. HARRISON SMITH, R.N. Maps and Illustrations. Crown 8vo, cloth, 7s. 6d.

THE ECHO says:—" For those who are at all

interested in the politics and the future of the Abyssinian kingdom, this record will be of the greatest value."

STATHAM, F. REGINALD—

POEMS AND SONNETS. By F. REGINALD STATHAM. Crown 8vo, cloth, 5s.

MR. MAGNUS. By F. REGINALD STATHAM. Crown 8vo, cloth, 6s.

This is a tale dealing with the daily life, political and social, of the town of Camberton, a ruby-mining centre in a British colony, where the financial genius of Mr. Magnus has succeeded in amalgamating and securing absolute control over all the interests concerned in the industry. The action takes place within one week, and the actors include Mr. Magnus, the officials of the Company, their employees and the general population of the town. The main thread of the plot is supplied by the adventures of two young men, Philip Winter and Raymond Wolston, who have accepted employment under the Company, the latter of whom has been made the object of a malevolent plot, contrived under the peculiar provisions of the law relating to the trade in rubies. The story is full of exciting and characteristic incidents—a public meeting in connection with the approaching election; an attack made on the post-office with a view to carrying off the weekly shipment of rubies; a visit to the underground workings in the mine; the collapse of a shaft and the threatened imprisonment of the miners; the heroic death of Edward Moore, a miner who sacrifices himself in order to facilitate the escape of his comrades; and the death, from natural causes, of Mr. Magnus himself. A charming feature in the story is supplied by the figure of Nelly, Raymond Wolston's sister, who undertakes a journey from England with the view of assisting her brother.

THEAL, GEORGE McCALL—

LIST OF MR. THEAL'S WORKS.

SOUTH AFRICA. By GEORGE McCALL THEAL, LL.D. Being Vol. XXXVIII. of

The Story of the Nations. Large crown 8vo, cloth, 5s.

IN PREPARATION.

THE PORTUGUESE IN SOUTH AFRICA. With a Description of the Native Races between the River Zambesi and the Cape of Good Hope during the Sixteenth Century.

WILMOT, Hon. A.—

THE STORY OF THE EXPANSION OF SOUTH AFRICA. By the Hon. A. WILMOT, Member of the Legislative Council, Cape of Good Hope. Second and Enlarged Edition. With Map, cloth, 5s.

THE TIMES says that this history—"Gives a summary at once lucid, instructive, and authoritative of South African history from the earliest times of European occupation to the present day. . . . Mr. Wilmot writes candidly and dispassionately."

IN PREPARATION.

MONOMOTAPA (RHODESIA). Its Monuments and its History from the most Ancient Times to the present Century. By the Hon. A. WILMOT. With Preface by H. RIDER HAGGARD. With Maps and Plates.

WORKMAN, FANNY B. & WM. H.

ALGERIAN MEMORIES: A Bicycle Tour over the Atlas to the Sahara. By FANNY B. WORKMAN and WM H. WORKMAN. 23 Illusts. Crown 8vo, cloth, 6s.

"There is plenty of readable matter in this well-written volume."—LITERARY WORLD.

"It is vastly interesting."
—BLACK AND WHITE.